Muddle Farm

Tasha Pym
Illustrated by Anni Axworthy

I went to Muddle Farm.

All the dogs said **Quack!**

All the ducks said **Woof!**

All the horses said **Cluck!**

All the chickens said **Neigh!**

All the cows said **Baaa!**

All the sheep said **Mooo!**

I went to tell the farmer.

He said . . .